AUSTRALIAN
Tropical Birds

A Selected Portfolio
by
Clifford & Dawn Frith

seate Tern

Designed & published in Australia
by **FRITH & FRITH** Books
'Prionodura', P.O. Box 581,
Malanda, Queensland 4885
Telephone (070) 96 8105
Facsimile (070) 96 8316

National Library of Australia
Card Number ISBN 0 9589942 1 8

First printed 1985
Second printing 1986
Third printing 1989
Fourth printing 1995

Other books in this series:
Australian Tropical Reptiles and Frogs
Australian Tropical Reef Life
Australian Tropical Butterflies
Australian Tropical Orchids
Australia's Cape York Peninsula
Australia's Wet Tropics Rainforest Life
Growing Australian Tropical Plants – Rainforest

To the memory of
Peggy Frith
in appreciation

Australian Peli

Preface

The success of our first book 'Australian Tropical Rainforest Life', published in 1983, clearly demonstrated the demand for modestly priced colourful and informative tropical natural history books of this type. We are particularly pleased to be able to publish the present book ourselves and, as was the case with 'Rainforest Life', to have it wholly produced in Australia.

Having devoted our first five years in tropical north Queensland to the study of birds and other life in tropical rainforests we have in recent years been finding some time to spend in other habitats north of Capricorn. The photographs seen in this little volume are a sample of some of the results of our work. Clearly, a book of this limited imagination and size can deal only very superficially with a selection of those birds occurring within the tropics. Many of the birds depicted in these pages are truly unique to the tropical regions of Australia, while others are more widespread over the continent but are, nevertheless, typical of the tropical avifauna. We have not attempted to include birds that are strictly confined to the Kimberley area of Western Australia, the Arnhem Land area of Northern Territory or the far western arid regions of Queensland because the vast majority of visitors to the tropics spend most of their time on eastern and north-eastern coastal Queensland. Given that we cannot present anything like a comprehensive coverage this seemed to be the most useful treatment. In a similar way we have been able to present only a small representation of those bird species typically found in each broad habitat type (see contents). Birds included in a particular habitat chapter are not necessarily found only in that habitat but may also occur in one or several additional habitats.

The most delightful aspect of our photographic activities over the past seven years has been meeting fine people we have come to know as friends. For hospitality, help in innumerable ways, and valued companionship in the field we are particularly grateful to Robyn and Rolly Clarke, Denise Coleman, Wendy and Bill Cooper, Gay Crowley, Graham Cumming, Phil and Joe Dowling, Stephen Garnett, Andrée Griffin, Annette, Bob, Marni and Brian McCullough, Rupert Russell, Rosalind and Arthur Sellars and Margaret and Arthur Thorsborne.

We thank Judy and Robbie Bredl, Barbara Bruce, Ian and Mavis Carter, Neil Dingwall, Evan Evans, Ea McLiesh, Susannah Russell, Linda and Bill Venn and John Young for locating birds and/or nests. Our good friends Daphne and Ralph Keller made available their delectable blind tower which has enabled us to reach and photograph some rare tropical birds at the nest. The Australian Bird Park, Cairns permitted us to photograph Grass Owls. The Queensland National Parks and Wildlife Service helped in various ways and we thank all staff, particularly Claude Azzopardi, Don Duffy, Brian King, Arthur Sellars, Andrew Taplin and John Winter.

Photo: W. T. Cooper

We are fortunate indeed that the photographic agency Australasian Nature Transparencies, or ANT, had been recently established in Melbourne as we were able to obtain from its files high quality slides of birds we have been unable to photograph. Those photographs not taken by us are fully credited beneath the picture.

All of our photographs were taken with OLYMPUS cameras, flash systems and accessories. A few pictures herein were taken with Olympus OM 2n cameras, but the great majority were obtained with the OM-4 camera body which incorporates a number of highly innovative technological advances particularly advantageous to wildlife work. Zuiko lenses from 35mm wide angle to the new 350mm F2.8, sometimes converted to 500mm with the 1.4X-A teleconverter, were used. Olympus camera systems and Olympus and Metz flash systems were supplied by R. Gunz Pty. Ltd., of Sydney, with particular thanks to Rolf Barme and Bob Pattie. The vast majority of film used was Kodachrome 64 KR135. ☐

Clifford and Dawn Frith,
Paluma, Tropical North Queensland

1

Introduction

The Tropics and the World of Birds

When considering the world of birds the term 'the tropics' invariably leads to thoughts of spectacularly colourful and perhaps even bizarre birds or bird groups. Certainly such a widespread association is understandable because many of the more gaudy and remarkable families of birds are in fact predominantly restricted to the tropics. Many of the more brightly coloured pigeons are tropical, as are the majority of the much loved parrots and the beautiful kingfishers, hornbills and their close relatives; and the remarkable toucans of South America. Among the smaller birds the particularly colourful pittas, cotingas, manakins, flowerpeckers, sunbirds, orioles, bowerbirds and birds of paradise are very predominantly tropical. To learn more of some of these bird groups a general book on birds of the world need be consulted (see page 69). Of course the tropics are biologically more diverse and rich than temperate regions and thus support more varied life forms which in part accounts for the diversity in form and colour amongst the birds of hotter climes. Many particularly colourful birds are rainforest dwelling and as this dense and complex habitat is very shaded bright colours (and vocalizations) doubtless prove invaluable aids to social communication between members of a bird species. Of course there are many exceptions to the rule; drab tropical birds and brightly coloured temperate ones.

The keen Australian birdwatcher must travel north of the Tropic of Capricorn if many of our more colourful and interesting species are to be seen. Often they are more interesting simply because they are so little known, due to their relative inaccessibility. Of approximately 725 species of birds recorded in Australia and adjacent seas about 117 can be seen only north of Capricorn. Another 50 species of Australian birds occur very predominantly within the tropics only, and an additional 321 species are widely distributed both within and south of the tropics. Thus the tropical zone, considerably less than half of the Australian land mass supports 488 birds species or sixty seven per cent of our avifauna. Of the birds illustrated in the following pages 43 are confined exclusively to the tropics, 23 are very predominantly limited to the tropics and 31 are widespread outside the tropics but are nevertheless also typical of the habitats under which they appear within the tropics. Of the habitats dealt with in this book only tropical rainforest is strictly confined to the tropics, therefore a larger proportion of rainforest birds appear in this book.

The seven types of country, or habitat, we deal with here are only very broad categories as a convenient arrangement facilitating the presentation of birds from similar environments. To fully take account of finer differences in habitats is beyond the scope or requirements of this publication.

Family Tree of Bird Life

Ornithologists, those that study birds in a scientific wa generally agree that there are some 9,000 species of birds living on earth. For our convenience all these birds whic collectively make up the Class AVES within the Kingdom ANIMALIA are categorized into twenty-seven groups called Orders. Each order of birds contains members mo closely related to each other than to birds in other orders Of course as in all classes of animals there are those that are more specialized than others. The twenty-seven orde of birds are divided into two basic groups; the non-passerines which are more 'primitive' birds which, as a generalization, do not perch or perch well; and the passerines which are the more advanced 'perching' birds The order Passeriformes is a vast assemblage of diverse families of birds that contains more than half of the worl bird species.

The remaining twenty-six orders of living birds constitute the non-passerines which include the flightles ratites, the pigeons (Order Columbiformes), the parrots (Psittaciformes) and other less easily defined orders such as the Pelecaniformes which includes not only the pelica but also the tropicbirds, boobies and gannets, cormorant darters and frigatebirds which are of course more closely related to the pelicans than to other birds but which form separate families within the order Pelecaniformes.

A bird family is, in turn, made up of one to many smaller units of very closely related birds called the genu or genera. The members of each genus consists of a number of species. For example, the Laughing Kookabur *Dacelo gigas*, and the only other member of its genus in Australia, the Blue-winged Kookaburra *Dacelo leachii*, ar both members of the genus *Dacelo* because they are clear more closely related to each other than to other members of the kingfisher family — Alcedinidae. They are both go species, distinct from each other, because they do not interbreed where they occur together. The species is the most important unit of the natural classification of living things. Members of a species breed only with other members of their species.

We use here mostly the common and scientific names given in Graham Pizzey's 'A Field Guide to the Birds of Australia' because it is very widely used by people interested in Australian birds, and because most of the names used are sensible.

A small map at the top of the text for each bird species provides a quick rough indication of the bird's distribution.

Lowland Tropical Rainforest

Orange-footed Scrubfowl
Megapodius reinwardt

Confined strictly to the tropics within Australia, this fascinating bird is widespread across the islands from the New Hebrides, Solomon Islands, New Guinea and Moluccas to the Philippines, Borneo, Lesser Sunda Islands, Java and the Nicobar Islands in the Indian Ocean. This bird together with the Brush Turkey (below) and the Malleefowl, *Leipoa ocellata*, of dry southern Australia constitute the Australian members of the bird family Megapodidae or mound-builders, so named because the males of most species accumulate huge mounds of vegetation or sand by scratching with their large feet. These mounds are incubator nests, in which the females will lay their eggs for the male to subsequently care for by maintaining the temperature and humidity within the mound at the optimum for incubation by adding or subtracting mound material with changes in climate.

The Scrubfowl is very vocal, producing weird and wonderful crows, cries and screams often through the night and is very familiar to visitors to Magnetic, Hinchinbrook and Dunk Islands and all of the rainforested tropical coast.

Brush-turkey
Alectura lathami

This is another megapode or mound-builder (see above) but is more widespread and familiar, occurring in both highland and lowland rainforests. They are commonly seen in picnic areas and gardens where they will eat almost anything. As in the Orange-footed Scrubfowl, males build large mounds in which the females lay their eggs. These birds feed rather like domestic fowls, scraping away leaf litter with their feet and pecking. The tail of the Brush-turkey is remarkable in being on a vertical axis, which it opens and closes during social encounters possibly to indicate dominance or submissiveness. In far northern populations the normally yellow wattle, larger in males, is purple.

Southern Cassowary
Casuarius casuarius

This huge flightless bird (opposite) is a remnant of the avian past, a primitive bird known as a ratite as are the New Zealand Kiwis, Ostriches of Africa, Rheas of South America and our familiar Emu.

The heavy dense plumage, horny casque atop the skull, and three to five odd and huge wire-like feather quills that extend from the vestigial wings are believed to provide protection for the bird in the dense tropical lowland and upland rainforests from Paluma, just north of Townsville, to northern Cape York Peninsula and New Guinea. As it runs quickly through the forest the head is lowered, casque first, and plumage and wing quills are held out to brush aside impeding foliage.

Female cassowaries, which are larger than males, are promiscuous and lay eggs in several male nests each year only to leave the male with the family duties.

Photo: R. & D. Keller/ANT

4

Purple-crowned Pigeon
Ptilinopus superbus

Seen here is a male Purple-crowned Pigeon on his nest and young one. This lovely bird is one of seven of Australia's twenty-two native pigeons that are known as fruit pigeons. The photograph gives the impression that this colourful bird would be conspicuous anywhere, even in its lush green rainforest home. In fact even these brightly coloured males, much more resplendent than their generally green mates that only sport a deep plum-purple patch on their rear crown, are most difficult to see. Their deep repeated 'whoop' call note is often heard in lowland and highland rainforest but birds are seldom seen until flushed into their whirring-winged flight.

Papuan Frogmouth
Podargus papuensis

Most people with even the slightest interest in wildlife about them are familiar with the Tawny Frogmouth, *Podargus strigoides*. Its larger Papuan relative is, however, confined to our tropical rainforests and other dense tropical vegetation. In place of the striking yellow iris of its commoner relative, the Papuan Frogmouth has a deep blood red iris. Frogmouths are closely related to owls but are members of a different family of birds and as such are quite different. Their feet are quite small and very weak, being adapted for perching and not at all helpful in snatching prey as are the powerful talons of owls. As their name implies, these birds have a huge mouth, used to snap up prey of large insects, frogs, lizards, mice and other small animals from the ground and vegetation.

Palm Cockatoo
Probosciger aterrimus

This, the largest species of cockatoo (opposite), is widespread through New Guinea and, fortunately, occurs in the great New Guinea-like lowland rainforest of northern Cape York Peninsula, where it is not uncommon. As its huge and immensely powerful bill suggests, it feeds on the seeds of particularly tough fruits and nuts. It has been seen to perform most acrobatic displays involving crest raising, flapping of extended wings and leaning forward over a perch to hang almost inverted. Very recently a remarkable observation of birds displaying at a potential tree-hollow nesting site by banging the hollow bough with a piece of wood held in the foot, as a tool, has been made; being another rare instance of tool-using in birds.

These birds fetch small fortunes in the illegal and deplorable live bird trade which is undoubtedly placing severe pressures on some populations in Irian Jaya and perhaps New Guinea. Australia, too, is not without such pressure but hopefully the very limited areas of rainforest supporting these birds are sufficiently protected and policed to ensure their survival.

Double-eyed Fig Parrot
Psittaculirostris diophthalma

This beautiful little bird is Australia's smallest parrot. The picture shows a male, with much red about the face, and a female feeding on their basic diet of cluster figs. This bird has three distinct isolated populations down the east coast of Australia from Cape York Peninsula to northern New South Wales. The southern population is now quite rare because of diminishing rainforest areas. The northern population is referred to as Marshall's Fig Parrot which the photograph, taken at Iron Range, depicts.

The central population of this species occurs from Paluma, just north of Townsville, northward to Cooktown in lowland and mountain rainforest and is that most commonly seen by bird watchers as it is present in tourist-frequented areas such as Paluma and the Atherton Tableland. In this population males have less red than the illustrated bird, and females have a red patch on forehead and a buff, as opposed to yellow, cheek area.

Pale-yellow Robin
Tregellasia capito

This appealing little robin, second smallest in Australia, occurs in two quite separate isolated populations on the east Australian coast. The southern population is confined to extreme south-eastern Queensland and north-eastern New South Wales whilst the northern one, pictured here, is found only from about the Townsville area northward nearly to Cooktown. Throughout its range this bird primarily associates with rainforest, and denser vegetation on watercourses. It is seen in gardens abutting rainforest and birds will venture onto lawns and flower beds to chase insect prey; more so during the dry winter months. It typically uses vertical sapling trunks to perch while surveying the ground for animal movement. It appears to associate closely with Lawyer Vine, or wait-a-while, when nesting and uses the viciously spiked main stems of these to nest build on, thereby attaining some defence from nest predators. In northern Cape York Peninsula rainforests this robin is replaced by the smallest of species the White-faced Robin, *Tregellasia leucops*, which is similar in general habits.

 ## Buff-breasted Paradise Kingfisher
Tanysiptera sylvia

This truly spectacular kingfisher has recently been given its unwieldy common name to replace the better known White-tailed Kingfisher. Of the ten kinds of Australian kingfisher it is undoubtedly the most spectacular. It is one of eight paradise kingfishers a group constituting the genus *Tanysiptera*, most members of which occur in New Guinea and surrounding islands. Australia's tropical lowland rainforests are much enhanced every year by this beautifully feathered bird which migrates south from New Guinea to breed in Australia. The birds arrive in early November and noisily establish small territories which must contain the bulbous termite mounds, usually on the ground, in which they will excavate a tunnel and nest chamber. The females, which have shorter tails, incubate the eggs and are then assisted in feeding one to three noisy young as they ceaselessly beg for insects, spiders, leeches, frogs and lizards. Young leave the nest in January and February quite capable of adequate flight. Once their offspring are independent of them the adult birds return to New Guinea, leaving the young birds to find their own way northward several weeks later.

Often residents of the far north, where this lovely bird occurs, mistakenly identify a glimpsed bird as a parrot because of its remarkable colouration. It is, however, very much a kingfisher; as is our famous kookaburra.

Yellow-breasted Boatbill
Machaerirhynchus flaviventer

This very rarely photographed little bird is the most peculiar of our Australian monarch flycatchers (see page 30); its very broad flattened beak being a quite unique adaptation, apparently for snatching flying insects in its tropical rainforest habitat. Not strictly confined to the lowlands, this strikingly plumaged flycatcher may be heard and seen in the upland rainforests and can be found to be fairly common in places, Its tiny suspended nest is, however, extremely difficult to find and as it may be built between four to twenty metres above ground, a lot of luck is required to locate one low enough to study and photograph. Seen here is the male bird; the female is a much lighter and duller yellow and is olive on the back where he is black.

Photo: R. & D. Keller/AN

Yellow Oriole
Oriolus flavocinctus

Of the two typical Australian orioles the Yellow is the truly tropical species, inhabiting predominantly lowland forests and mangroves, also more open vegetation on occasions. It is a very vocal bird and its quite powerful bubbling calls of several notes are characteristic where pairs of birds are resident. Unlike the Figbird (see page 58), which is also a member of the oriole family, the Yellow Oriole does not flock but may be nomadic when not breeding. On the east Queensland coast it is necessary to travel as far north as about Townsville to enter the breeding range of this oriole, which constructs its hammock-like suspended nest from two to sixteen metres above ground. It feeds almost exclusively on tropical fruits, but doubtless feeds young birds some insect foods.

Graceful Honeyeater
Meliphaga gracilis

This exclusively tropical honeyeater (see page 20) together with the very closely related Yellow-spotted Honeyeater, *Meliphaga notata*, of identical distribution, and the far more widespread Lewin's Honeyeater, *M. lewinii*, present a serious identification problem. All three are of similar appearance, the Lewin's being significantly larger and more easily differentiated than the other two. Where all three occur together, however, problems can be encountered unless calls are heard or more than one species can be seen together for comparison. The Lewin's tends, however, to be more a highland species in the tropics. The Graceful and Yellow-spotted Honeyeaters are particularly similar but the former is a little smaller, paler below and has a proportionally longer and slimmer bill than the latter. The yellow ear mark spot of the Lewin's is larger and less round than in its smaller relatives, and it has a grey, not a brown, eye.

The Graceful Honeyeater is predominantly a lowland tropical rainforest bird but also inhabits other denser vegetation and thickets, and woodlands, orchards and gardens. It feeds on fruit and insects in addition to flower nectar.

Helmeted Friarbird
Philemon buceroides

Another exclusively tropical bird, the Helmeted Friarbird, occurs in Arnhem Land and from the top of Cape York Peninsula down the east coast to the Tropic of Capricorn. Of the other three species of friarbirds, the Silver-crowned, *Philemon argenticeps*, is also exclusively tropical, but of wider distribution. In addition to lowland rainforests the Helmeted Friarbird also occupies mangroves, denser riverine vegetation, open forests and woodlands. A large honeyeater, up to thirty-seven centimetres in length, this bird is both impressive and noisy as it feeds upon the nectar of tree blossom; often forming squawking congregations of several dozen birds.

Shining Starling
Aplonis metallica

This lovely bird (page 12), also called the Metallic Starling, is the only member of the large old-world starling family native to Australia; the Common Starling and Mynah being introduced pests. It is widespread through New Guinea, the Solomons and Moluccas, but in Australia is a migratory visitor to tropical extreme north and eastern coastal Queensland only.

Like the majority of starlings it is very social and flocks of thousands of birds frequent lowland rainforests, mangroves, woodlands and gardens in search of fruits. It is also highly gregarious when nesting, breeding in small to large colonies. The vast majority of starlings nest in tree holes or crevices in trees or buildings, but the Shining Starling and a few close relatives build huge hanging pear-shaped nests of twigs and tendrils suspended from a tree branch with a side entrance sometimes partly obscured by a funnel or spout. Colonies may involve hundreds of nests built so close together that they appear as one huge structure.

Upland
Tropical
Rainforest

Red-necked Rail
Rallina tricolor

Whilst this rainforest-dwelling rail (opposite) is rare and restricted in range within Australia it is widespread through New Guinea, the Moluccas and the Bismark Archipelago where it is as little known as it is here. Certainly birds in the Paluma and Atherton Tableland areas are resident throughout the year, but other birds apparently leave Australia in winter for New Guinea. Like so many rails this is a difficult bird to see well, particularly in its very dense habitat. It may often be heard, however, as it produces a very loud repeated series of sharp 'keck' notes which diminish in power and clarity; usually given at dawn and dusk or during very overcast dark weather. Immature birds lack the rich reddish plumage and are predominantly greyish.

Crimson Rosella
Platycercus elegans

This familiar and popular bright parrot is widespread through much of south-east Queensland, New South Wales, Victoria and eastern South Australia but a population of smaller and darker red birds is quite isolated and restricted to the tropical upland rainforests from Eungella northward almost to Cooktown. These northern birds are not as confiding as the southern ones which may occur in more open habitats than their tropical relations and often become tame at picnic areas. Food consists of seeds but fruits, berries, buds, shoots, blossom and some insects are taken. On the edge of tropical rainforest this bird is commonly seen eating the seeds of the sarsaparilla tree which vigorously colonizes the edges of roads and clearings cut into the forest.

Bassian Thrush
Zoothera lunulata

A widespread population of birds previously known as White's or Scaly Thrush, distributed from the Atherton Tableland down the Australian east coast to Victoria, Tasmania and eastern South Australia, was in 1983 demonstrated to include two different species. The Bassian Thrush occurs in two forms, one in South Australia, Victoria and Tasmania, eastern New South Wales and south-eastern Queensland and another, the one illustrated, in the highland rainforests of the Atherton Region (see page 16). The other species, now known as the Russet-tailed Thrush, *Z. heinei*, occurs in north-eastern New South Wales and south-eastern central coast and north-eastern Queensland where it meets the Bassian Thrush. The two species have differing calls and the Russet-tailed Thrush has a shorter tail, rufous-tinged rump, and russet tail but they are nevertheless very similar in appearance. The Bassian Thrush is a shy ground-frequenting thrush that feeds singly or in pairs on insects, worms, other invertebrates and fruit.

Spectacled Monarch Flycatcher
Monarcha trivirgatus

The Spectacled Monarch Flycatcher is not confined to the tropics, almost reaching Sydney in New South Wales (see page 30), but it is a bird very typical of tropical rainforest environments. Further south on the east coast it also associates with wet forests and adjacent drier woodlands where its noisy chattering calls are conspicuous and characteristic. In this monarch flycatcher the sexes are similar in appearance, although females are somewhat duller in their colours than males (which is the sex illustrated here). These active birds can be seen singly or in pairs in the middle and lower levels of the rainforest where they flutter and hop through the foliage in search of insects. The nest is typically constructed in the fork of a small sapling or between vine stems and usually two young are raised.

Grey-headed Robin
Poecilodryas albispecularis

Many Australian robins (not true robins at all but members of the flycatcher group) are brightly coloured in strong reds, pinks or yellows, but the Grey-headed Robin is as beautiful and striking in a more subtle range of tortoiseshell hues. This large robin, like so many unique Australian rainforest birds, is confined to that small part of our tropics known as the Atherton Region. It occurs in highland rainforest, above about two hundred metres above sea level, between Paluma and the Bloomfield River region. In the Paluma rainforest, at one thousand metres above sea level, they would be the most numerous bird, their monotone single oft-repeated whistle note being a characteristic of these areas. This bird's closest relative, the White-browed Robin *Poecilodryas superciliosa*, occurs through much of the tropics in rainforest, riverine forests, swamps, woodlands, pandanus thickets and mangroves.

Noisy Pitta
Pitta versicolor

The pitta family consists of twenty-eight colourful birds which occur from Africa through South East Asia, Indonesia, and Australasia to some South Pacific Islands. Australia has three resident pitta species and a fourth, the Blue-winged, *Pitta moluccensis*, has been recorded only a couple of times as a vagrant to north-western Australia. Two of our three resident species are somewhat inaccessible, the Rainbow Pitta, *P. iris*, being confined to the Kimberley and Arnhem Land regions of West Australia and Northern Territory respectively; and the Red-bellied Pitta, *P. erythrogaster*, to the extreme northern tip of the Cape York Peninsula. The lovely Noisy Pitta (opposite), however, occurs in rainforests and other wet dense forests from northern Cape York Peninsula to Sydney, New South Wales. It lives on the forest floor and feeds upon animals in the leaf litter and some small fruits. It can often be attracted into one's sight by giving its loud and clear 'walk-to-work' whistle.

Fernwren
Crateroscelis gutturalis

This diminutive bird of the tropical highland rainforest floor is distributed over an even smaller area of the Atherton Region than is the Grey-headed Robin (see page 16) as it occurs only above six hundred metres above sea level. Whilst it is quite vocal, producing very high pitched drawn out whistles and scolding notes, it is rather retiring and difficult to see unless by a lone and patient observer. It hops actively over the forest floor leaf litter turning over individual leaves and small amounts of debris with its fine tweezer-like bill in search of small animal foods. A remarkable aspect of this bird's breeding is its relatively huge and solid domed nest of rootlets and mosses which is attached to a tree trunk, bank or small cave wall and in which two white eggs are laid. We believe this may be the first photograph published of this species at its nest.

Northern Logrunner
Orthonyx spaldingii

One of only two species of logrunner the Chowchilla or Northern Logrunner is a very different bird than its more widespread and smaller relative of eastern New South Wales and extreme south-eastern Queensland. The Northern Logrunner lives in tropical highland and lowland rainforests of the Atherton Region. These extremely vocal birds, in which the female has a rufous breast as seen here and the male has it white, are active on the forest floor. They hop and run about in small flocks of about six to eight birds and defend a territory by calling along its perimeter. They feed by grasping leaf litter in one foot and throwing it away from them to one side whilst visually searching intently for animals to snatch up in the bill. In order to do this comfortably without falling off the single leg left supporting them they have a remarkably modified tail which acts as a prop, rather like we use a shooting stick. The central shafts of the tail feathers have been thickened into very strong spines, which give the bird the alternative name of Spalding's Spinetail. Leaning back and down onto this useful support the bird can obtain leverage to tear and pull at the forest floor. A frantically feeding bird is amusing to watch, as it continuously hurls debris about itself, appearing to almost drop out of sight beneath the litter.

Bower's Shrike-thrush
Colluricincla boweri

Of the four Australian shrike-thrushes the largest, the Grey, *Colluricincla harmonica*, is by far the best known as it occurs throughout the country and is a familiar garden bird. Bower's Shrike-thrush (opposite), on the other hand, is hardly known at all as it is confined to the mountain tropical rainforests of the Atherton Region where it is a difficult bird to see notwithstanding its loud chuck and whistle call notes. At forest edges this bird occurs together with the Rufous Shrike-thrush, *C. megarhyncha*, from which it can be differentiated by its blackish bill and less white throat.

Macleay's Honeyeater
Xanthotis macleayana

Yet another bird of restricted range from Cooktown south to Paluma; on the rainforested ranges and rainforest, woodland and riverine vegetation of the lowlands. This is one of Australia's sixty-eight honeyeaters, a family of one hundred and seventy species in the Australasian Region, which forms one of Australia's most characteristic bird groups. As the name implies, they frequently feed on flower nectar; and many species are important to native flowering plants as pollinators. In rainforest Macleay's Honeyeater is not an easy bird to see well because it is quieter than many honeyeaters. It is most commonly encountered singly or in pairs and spends much time in the canopy of the forest, although it will enter orchards and gardens and quickly comes to frequent bird tables.

Bridled Honeyeater
Lichenostomus frenatus

This is primarily a bird of tropical highland rainforests, although it can be seen at some lowland rainforest locations such as at Cape Tribulation. It also occurs in wet forests along watercourses, swamp woodlands, and in drier forests adjacent to rainforests. Like many honeyeaters it is very active, vocal, and aggressive. Birds can sometimes be seen pressing home vigorous attacks upon another, and birds gripping each other and tumbling down to bump onto the forest floor are not infrequently observed in the breeding season. This bird is particularly fond of taking nectar from flowering climbing pandanus and the Umbrella Tree. This northern honeyeater would have to be described as very little known, but it is remarkable to note here that this bird's closest relative, the Eungella Honeyeater, *Lichenostomus hindwoodi*, was discovered in the very heavily visited rainforest at Eungella, near Mackay, in Queensland in 1977 where it had been overlooked as being the Bridled Honeyeater for many years. Whilst having a similar call to the Bridled the Eungella bird is, however, quite distinctly different in plumage.

Mountain Thornbill
Acanthiza katherina

Of the twelve thornbills in Australia the Mountain Thornbill is the only one confined to the tropics, where it is extremely restricted to the rainforested highlands of Paluma to near Cooktown above about four hundred metres above sea level. This bird was long thought of as merely a form of the widespread Brown Thornbill until it was pointed out in 1968 that it has distinctive white eyes. As no other similarly sized birds of potentially confusing character occur within its range with white eyes it is easily identified. It is a foliage foraging bird, actively searching for insects in small flocks in outer leaves of tree canopies. The birds at times produce sweet and melodius clear calls. The nest is a lovely compact dome of fine grasses and fibres decorated outside with mosses and lichens. The nest was not discovered until 1971 and the eggs not described until several years later.

Blue-faced Finch
Erythrura trichroa

This is undoubtedly by far the rarest and most restricted of all our nineteen native grass finches. It is a rarely seen bird and is, therefore, eagerly sought by keen bird watchers visiting the tropical rainforest areas of the Atherton Tableland and adjacent coastal areas of Queensland where the bird frequents rainforest and rainforest edges and mangrove fringes. It has been recorded as present on the Atherton Tableland throughout the year, but is somewhat unpredictable in its appearances which doubtless relates to the local availability of suitable seeding grasses. Recent sightings of this bird are few, and it has been suggested it is declining in numbers perhaps because of the increasing loss of rainforest and mangrove areas. Beyond Australia, however, this bird is widespread and occurs throughout much of the South Pacific Islands, New Guinea and the Moluccas. The rump and upper tail of this bird, not visible in this photograph, are dark red. Far more widespread tropical finches are the Crimson, Star, Masked, Long-tailed, Gouldian (page 56), Yellow-rumped and Pictorella.

Spotted Catbird
Ailuroedus melanotis

Of Australia's nine truly fascinating bowerbirds (see also pages 59 & 67) the two catbirds are the least remarkable. Both the Green Catbird, *Ailuroedus crassirostris*, of sub-tropical and temperate rainforests of the south-eastern corner of Queensland and eastern New South Wales and the Spotted Catbird (opposite) of the tropical rainforests are typical birds in their reproductive behaviour inasmuch as a male and female, which are identical, pair for at least one breeding season and defend a territory in which they share the duties of raising the young. In this respect they are unlike most bowerbirds, in which males are promiscuous bower builders and females have to raise their young away from, and unaided by, the males. Catbirds are named for their cat-like wailing calls. They predominantly eat fruits but parent birds feed their young a good deal of worms, insects and nestlings of smaller birds.

Tooth-billed Bowerbird
Scenopoeetes dentirostris

Adult male tooth-bills clear a small patch of rainforest floor, several square metres in area, of all leaf litter and debris and then decorate this conspicuous area with leaves placed paler underside uppermost to produce maximum contrast. This is the male's 'court' at which he loudly sings, typically mimicking the calls of numerous other rainforest species, in order to attract females. The visiting females must be suitably impressed by his court and decorations, his vocalizations and his displays, if they are to mate with him. With courting and mating over, females depart to lay their one or two eggs and raise the subsequent young entirely unaided.

This vocal but retiring and difficult-to-see bowerbird is found in tropical upland rainforests of the Atherton Region usually over six hundred metres above sea level. Both sexes are identically cryptically coloured.

Golden Bowerbird
Prionodura newtoniana

Golden Bowerbirds have a very restricted range, being confined to the tropical rainforests higher than about nine hundred metres above sea level, from just south of Cooktown southward to Paluma. It is the world's smallest bowerbird, about the size of a Common Starling, but builds the largest of bowers. The mature male (page 24) is a brilliant golden-yellow and his unique feather structure refracts light which often produces pure white highlights on the plumage. Adult males probably do not attain their golden plumage until after their sixth or seventh year, and until then have the appearance of females. Their bower usually consists of one or two towers of sticks up to three metres tall with a display perch protruding from a single tower bower, or connecting the two towers. The sticks of the towers where they meet this display perch are more skilfully laid and it is on these that decorations are placed.

Females are dressed in greys and olive-brown to render them far less conspicuous whilst raising one or two young in a small cup nest in a tree crevice.

23

Mangroves
& Mudflats

Plumed Egret
Egretta intermedia

The Plumed or Intermediate Egret occupies approximately half of Australia involving the north of the western tropics, the eastern tropics and much of the central-east and south-east of the continent. This bird is so named because during the breeding season it has a spectacular spray of long fine lacy plumes on the back and breast. Some other egrets also have such breeding plumage. The Plumed Egret is commoner in the north of Australia than the south-east and frequents shallow waters as well as mudflats and mangroves in which it has been observed to breed. It is also to be seen feeding in pastures. It feeds upon fish and other aquatic animals, and upon large insects and particularly grasshoppers. This egret also lives through much of Africa, throughout India, South East Asia and southern New Guinea. It is a bird that nests in colonies and almost invariably with other water bird species.

Mangrove Heron
Butorides striatus

This bird has a coastal distribution around some two thirds of the Australian coastline, but has a vast distribution in a global context. It is found throughout North America, Middle America, Galapagos Islands, and most of South America, most of Africa, the Indian Ocean Islands, India, South East Asia, China, Japan, Indonesia and the South Pacific Islands. Over this extensive range it has evolved many local forms so that ornithologists presently recognise some thirty subspecies or races. In Australia two conspicuously different plumages of the bird occur, the typical darker bird seen here, and a rufous-red form in north-western West Australia. It associates closely with mangroves and mudflats but also frequents other salt waterways and exposed reefs.

Pied Stilt
Himantopus himantopus

Stilts belong to a family of birds, including the avocets, consisting of seven species that are perfectly adapted for life in wetlands, with extremely long delicate legs. The Pied Stilt has an almost world-wide distribution and is known outside Australia by the name of Black-winged Stilt. It is at home in both fresh and brackish water and so may be seen in lagoons, flood plains, rivers, lake edges, estuaries and mudflats. Its food consists of aquatic plants and animals which are obtained as the bird wades through the water with its long bill held vertically or nearly so. It is a sociable bird and may be seen in small groups to flocks of many hundreds. In flight the pink legs trail well beyond the tail and are apparently used in flight as the tail is normally used.

Beach Stone-curlew
Burhinus neglectus

The Beach Stone-curlew belongs to the same family as the Bush Stone-curlew (page 64), the Burhinidae, a group consisting of only nine species world-wide. They are also known as thick knees because of the swollen 'knee' joints. As its name clearly suggests this is a bird of the coast, where it occurs on quieter beaches, reefs, sandflats, mudflats and mangroves. It is a striking but little known bird that will run ahead of one if disturbed, or take short flights with slow, slightly stiff, wing flaps. Whilst this bird may be seen actively feeding in the daytime most of its activity appears to be nocturnal. Moreover, a bird, or pairs of birds, are not infrequently flushed from the beach crest vegetation where they have clearly been sheltering from the heat of the day.

Torres Strait Pigeon
Ducula spilorrhoa

This is the pigeon of the more commonly known names of Nutmeg Pigeon or Torresian Imperial Pigeon. It is as fascinating as it is beautiful, being a bird that migrates annually to the Australian tropics from New Guinea, to arrive in mid-August and depart during February and March. In Queensland the bird nests in large colonies in mangrove forests and rainforests on offshore islands, in coastal mangroves on the mainland and sometimes in mainland rainforest and adjacent areas. The sexes of the pairs raising their single young on the islands take turns each day to fly to the mainland tropical rainforests for fruits (see page 39). Island breeding colonies used to be vandalized by sailors, and subsequently by trigger-happy day trippers but have recovered in recent years. The great threat to these colonies would be the loss of their mainland lowland rainforest feeding ground.

Mangrove Golden Whistler
Pachycephala melanura

A person unaware of the wholly tropical Mangrove Golden Whistler would inevitably mistake it for the far more widespread Golden Whistler, *Pachycephala pectoralis*, so familiar in Tasmania, eastern, south-eastern and south-western Australia. Other than mangroves, with which this species particularly associates, the bird is also to be found in patches of coastal rainforest, monsoon forest, and riverine vegetation as well as on vegetated coastal islands. Seen here is the male, far more colourful than his pale mate, feeding young at the nest.

Little Kingfisher
Ceyx pusillus

The Little Kingfisher (opposite), smaller than a House Sparrow, is the smallest of Australian kingfishers. It is confined to the tropics within Australia but also occurs in New Guinea, the Solomon Islands and the Moluccas where it frequents mangrove creeks and swamps as well as rainforests and dense scrubs particularly along well vegetated rivers and creeks. It closely associates with waterways and is one of only two Australian kingfishers, the other being the Azure *Ceyx azureus*, that live up to their names and typically dive into water for their prey. Other Australian kingfishers such as the kookaburras (page 53) feed on the land, on insects, reptiles and other animals. This brilliantly plumaged little bird is most commonly encountered alone, unless a breeding pair is seen together. The nest is a tunnel into a mud bank or termite mound which terminates in a small chamber where five to six eggs are laid.

Photo: G. A. Cummin

Shining Flycatcher
Myiagra alecto

This very attractive species is one of a group of twelve birds known collectively as monarch flycatchers. Of these the Yellow-breasted Boatbill (page 10), Black-winged, Pied and Frilled Monarch Flycatchers, and the Broad-billed Flycatcher are exclusively tropical, three more species are nearly so, and the other four are more widespread. The Shining Flycatcher is very nearly wholly tropical and within its range is always associated closely with water most often in mangroves, but also in rainforest patches, riverine vegetation and paperbark and pandanus swamps. It is a very vocal bird and quickly attracts attention by its sharp grating or insect-like rasping calls. When calling, the resplendent male often widely opens his bill to expose the brilliant orange of his mouth interior in striking contrast to his highly glossed blue-black plumage. Females (below) on the other hand are strikingly tri-coloured with a head the colour of males but with snowy white underparts and rich chestnut, or rufous back, wings and tail.

Shining Flycatchers share the nesting duties between the sexes, both birds partaking in the building of a firm little cup-shaped nest of bark pieces, vines and tendrils and spiderwebs, decorated with lichen and moss on the outside. They share the incubation of two or three spotted and blotched pale blue or green eggs and the feeding of the young. Their diet consists predominantly of insects but tiny crustaceans and shellfish are taken from mangrove muds.

Outside Australia Shining Flycatchers occur in the Moluccas and in New Guinea and surrounding islands.

Black Butcherbird
Cracticus quoyi

Of the eight Australian members of the butcherbird family, which includes our familiar magpies, currawongs and butcherbirds, only two are exclusive to the tropics. These are the Black-backed Butcher, *Cracticus mentalis*, of northern Cape York Peninsula and the largest of the group the Black Butcherbird. This bird has an immensely large and powerful beak, viciously tipped with a hook, for capturing its animal foods of birds and their eggs, reptiles, frogs, insects, crustaceans and some fruits; in mangroves, rainforests, riverine forests and more open woodlands. Like its relatives, it often takes larger prey to a thorn or tree crevice to spike or wedge it in order to be able to tear it into manageable pieces for itself or its young. Interestingly, this bird has two colour forms, some birds having a rufous colour throughout with some blackish barring below. The two young in the nest photographed here at Cardwell were in fact one of each colour. The loud yodelling calls of this bird are powerful and very characteristically far-carrying, sometimes amusing, sounds.

Yellow Honeyeater
Lichenostomus flavus

Australian honeyeaters have evolved and diversified in large part to take advantage of the nectar available from Australia's flowering flora, and the rich smaller insect life. They can be considered to some extent to be Australia's answer to the sunbirds of Africa and Asia (see page 56) and the hummingbirds of South America. Quite a few honeyeater species are confined to the tropical region. These include the Buff-breasted, White-lined, Varied, White-gaped, Yellow-tinted, Green-backed, White-streaked, Rufous-banded, Rufous-throated, Banded and Red-headed Honeyeaters.

The Yellow Honeyeater is a bold and inquisitive bird that really makes itself at home in busy parks and gardens, mangroves, riverine vegetation, eucalypt woodlands and rainforest edges.

Brown-backed Honeyeater
Ramsayornis modestus

This handsome small honeyeater (page 32), is confined to tropical eastern Queensland where it lives in coastal mangroves, adjacent paperbark swamp and riverine and swamp woodlands. It occurs singly, or in pairs and in small groups and during migration larger concentrations may be seen. The southernmost populations appear to migrate from the north, from Cape York Peninsula or New Guinea, in August and depart in April. They feed predominantly on insects but of course flower nectar, particularly from paperbarks, is important too. The suspended dome-shaped nest may be solitarily placed in foliage, often over water, or may be one of a nesting colony of up to twenty nests in a localized area. This bird lays two eggs but its nests are often parasitized by cuckoos which lay their eggs in the honeyeater's nest for this diminutive bird to incubate and then raise the highly demanding young cuckoo.

Barrier Reef Islands

Red-footed Booby
Sula sula

A truly tropical breeding seabird within Australia the Red-footed Booby also breeds throughout the shores and islands of the earth's tropical oceans where it feeds on crustaceans, squid and fishes. The two other boobies of our tropics are easily distinguished from this one (see page 37) and in Australian temperate coastal regions, the other member of this bird family, the Australian Gannet, *Morus serrator*, replaces the boobies. In addition to the white plumaged bird such as the individual seen here birds commonly occur with fawn coloured feathering, as do intermediate birds with varying amounts of fawn and white.

Frigatebirds

When not perched on the nest or elsewhere frigatebirds spend their entire lives in the air, their very long slender wings and tiny feet leaving them ill-adapted for walking, or for swimming on the surface of the sea for which their plumage is not water-proofed. The frigatebirds, of which there are five on earth, are often misleadingly but understandably referred to as sea hawks because they look and behave like birds of prey. It is common to see these extremely fast and agile fliers chasing other sea birds, twisting and turning after the fleeing bird and sometimes snapping at it with their long viciously hooked bill. The sea birds they chase have been identified by the frigatebirds as individuals obviously carrying a gullet full of food, usually toward their mate or young. The frigatebird will press home its attack until the laden bird regurgitates its load in order to more easily flee, leaving the parasitic frigatebird to feed upon its hard-earned meal. Chased birds too reluctant to disgorge their food have been seen to have their wing broken by a snapping pursuer. The male Great Frigatebird, *Fregata minor*, seen opposite, is displaying his inflated gular pouch, normally deflated and overlooked, in courtship display. This, the largest frigatebird species, is confined in Australia very predominantly to the Arnhem Land and Queensland coasts and breeds only within the tropics.

The smaller Lesser Frigatebird, *F. ariel*, seen here with a young on the nest, is more widespread in Australia; occurring throughout the entire tropical coast and on the east coast south of Capricorn to the extreme north-east corner of New South Wales. Again it is known only to breed within the tropics. In flight adult males of the two frigatebirds can be identified because the Greater is an entirely black bird whereas the Lesser has a small white patch on the inner wing against the body giving the appearance of white 'armpits'. The identification is more complex in females and juveniles.

Photo: B. King/QNPWS

Photo: B. King/QNPWS

Photo: B. King/QNPWS

Red-tailed Tropicbird
Phaethon rubricauda

The tern-like tropicbirds are in fact more closely related to the frigatebirds, cormorants, boobies and pelicans. Of the world's three tropicbird species only the Red-tailed breeds in Australia, predominantly on Raine Island where the photograph (opposite above) was taken. Notwithstanding odd records of this bird south of the tropics it occurs in Australia very predominantly within the tropics, as well as the tropical Indian and Pacific Oceans, where it feeds on fish and squid for which it dives into the sea.

Crested Tern
Sterna bergii

This large heavy-billed tern (left) is found throughout our coastline and is widespread through the tropical seas except those of South America. It is commonly seen on Barrier Reef Islands and a significant nesting colony occurs on tourist-frequented Michaelmas Cay off Cairns in Queensland. This tern feeds on fish for which it plunges onto the sea surface partly submerging itself.

Masked and Brown Boobies

Both of these boobies, can be seen in the picture of a Raine Island booby nesting colony at the bottom of the page opposite. The predominantly white birds with a small area of bare black facial skin are the Masked Boobies, *Sula dactylatra*, and the dark brown birds with white underparts are Brown Boobies, *S. leucogaster*. Both the Masked and Brown Boobies range through the tropical Atlantic, Pacific and Indian Oceans and feed upon fish, particularly flying fish and squid.

Silver Gull
Larus novaehollandiae

This seabird is found throughout most of the country; being a highly successful bird in adapting to man and his environs. On our tropical islands, however, it lives a thoroughly natural existence, feeding upon beach-washed marine animal life and during other seabird breeding seasons by pillaging eggs and young. The birds in this picture (left) are with two Banded Rails (see below) eating the eggs in a booby colony left unattended.

Banded Rail
Rallus philippensis

This rail is widespread over much of Australia and is associated with dense lush vegetation. On many of the Barrier Reef Islands, however, it occurs in extremely open and exposed situations supporting scant vegetation. On these islands they feed upon beach strand debris and animal life but vigorously predate hatchling seabirds and rob other birds' nests of very young chicks and eggs, as seen in the picture.

Sooty Tern
Sterna fuscata

This lovely tern of strongly contrasting monochrome plumage occurs throughout the tropical and subtropical Atlantic, Pacific and Indian Oceans but in Australia is very predominantly tropical. It breeds in large to vast colonies, very noisy places where frantic activity and screamings continue as long as disturbance by visitors is evident. Michaelmas Cay, offshore from Cairns, in north Queensland is undoubtedly the most regularly visited colony, as tour operators now take many daily visitors to a floating facility anchored off the cay. Unlike many terns which feed by directly plunging into the sea the Sooty Terns snatch their squid, fish and crustacean food from the sea surface in flight mostly at dusk, and at night. This bird also appears on the Contents page(i),and page 33.

Black-naped and Roseate Terns

The Black-naped Tern, *Sterna sumatrana* (right), occurs widely through tropical Indian and Pacific Oceans from Madagascar off east Africa to Samoa in the Pacific and is to be seen in Australia on the Arnhem Land, Gulf of Carpentaria and Queensland coasts to just south of Capricorn. It breeds in colonies, predominantly on inshore islands of the Great Barrier Reef where birds make a shallow scrape in coral and shingle beaches or lay their one to three eggs in rock crevices. The terns feed very predominantly on small fishes. The tourist-frequented Dunk and Heron Islands support breeding colonies.

The Roseate Tern, *S. dougallii* [left and page (ii)], is one of a number of very similar-looking species but it is the only one of them that beeds in Australia. The completely white and long tail streamers, extending well beyond the wing tips, help to identify this species. The Roseate is more widespread in Australia than the Sooty and the Black-naped, for it extends around the continent and down the West Australian coast almost to Perth. This is a colonial nester and will form large colonies of its own kind or will sometimes nest with the Black-naped or Fairy Terns *S. nereis*.

Torres Strait Pigeon
Ducula spilorrhoa

This pigeon also appears under the mangrove section (page 28) but we also illustrate it here as it is very seabird-like in appearance when seen with a Barrier Reef Island backdrop. It breeds on a number of the inner Barrier Reef islands from which it flies to and fro over the sea to the mainland in search of fruiting trees in rainforests. Flocks can be large and are always spectacular to watch, as they purposefully speed in direct and powerful flight.

Common Noddy
Anous stolidus

The Common Noddy, also pictured on the inside back cover, is one of the three noddy terns that occur in Australia, and it is the largest and by far the most widespread of them. Beyond Australia it nests on tropical and subtropical islands of the Pacific, Indian and Atlantic Oceans. One of the most visited nesting colonies of this species is on Michaelmas Cay, but it nests on numerous other oceanic and offshore islands. The nest is an untidy cup of vegetation lined with some shells and pebbles placed on the ground or on lower vegetation. One egg only is laid.

Wetlands

Pied Heron
Ardea picata

Of the fourteen herons found within Australia the Pied (page 41) is one of the only two species confined to breeding within the tropics, the other being the large Great-billed Heron, *Ardea sumatrana*. Outside Australia the Pied Heron can be seen in Borneo, the Celebes and through the islands of New Guinea. Within its tropical range the bird associates closely with swamps, lakes and lagoons and may also be seen on river margins, mudflats and in mangrove areas.

Little Pied Cormorant
Phalacrocorax melanoleucos

The Little Pied Cormorant is found throughout Australia, in suitable wetland habitats from coastal and estuarine situations to all inland waters, even very small dams and ponds. The other four cormorants in Australia are its closest relatives but then come the other members of its group within Australia, the Darter, boobies and frigatebirds (pages 34-37) and Pelican (below). Cormorants swim with head and neck upright and the body held low in the water and dive for their aquatic foods of fish, frogs and other life.

Australian Pelican
Pelecanus conspicillatus

This familiar huge bird [see also page (iii)] is much loved as a graceful swimming and flying bird, that becomes clumsy and awkward on its inadequate legs. Birds occur throughout Tasmania, and its mainland populations fluctuate dramatically in the interior with the availability of surface water. During drought the species will remain unseen for many years, only to appear in large numbers when substantial rains create suitable habitats. Its method of fishing, swimming in groups of birds which all plunge the head and neck into the water together to snatch up the encircled prey, is well known. Such birds swimming gracefully and moving in perfect unison appear to be performing a well choreographed aquatic dance, giving little indication of the serious business of making a living.

Black-necked Stork
Xenorhynchus asiaticus

This beautiful bird (opposite) is better known to most Australians as the Jabiru. It is one of seventeen stork species on earth and is the only Australian representative of that group of very large and huge-billed birds. It is distributed throughout the northern part of the tropics but on east coastal areas extends south of Capricorn almost to the Victorian border. Elsewhere, it is found from India through South East Asia, Indonesia to New Guinea. The Jabiru is a bird of swamplands, floodplains, mudflats and mangroves where it feeds upon fish, eels, frogs and other large aquatic life.

Large Egret
Egretta alba

This is the largest of the five egret species found in Australia in which all white plumages occur. Like the Plumed Egret (see page 26) it has a yellow bill and blackish legs and feet, but it is a much larger bird. It is, however, far more extensively distributed than is the Plumed Egret, and is in fact the most widespread of all the white egrets. This bird is closely associated with the shallow waters of swamps, lagoons, rivers, dams and irrigated areas where it most gracefully and patiently hunts for its foods of fish, amphibians, reptiles and insects.

Yellow-billed Spoonbill
Platalea flavipes

Spoonbills are quite obviously remarkable for their strange bill shape, which is of course very highly modified for a peculiar method of feeding. These large wading birds walk through the shallows with their bill in the water or mud and sweep the head and neck from side to side. The extremely sensitive spatulate tip of the bill is quick to respond to the touch of a crustacean, mollusc, insect or small fish which the bird then snaps up. Whilst both of Australia's Yellow-billed and Royal Spoonbills are all white they differ in leg, bill and facial colouration. The Royal Spoonbill, *P. regia*, has black legs and bill whereas those of the Yellow-billed are yellowish.

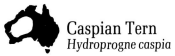

Caspian Tern
Hydroprogne caspia

This, the largest of terns, is considerably larger than the Silver Gull (see page 37) and has a bill of massive proportions. It is more widespread than any other tern in Australia, being found to occur at some time throughout all states of the country. It is a bird that feeds in both deep and shallow waters and catches its fish prey by diving into the water from up to thirteen metres high, often disappearing beneath the surface before reappearing with its catch. The bird seen here is in non-breeding plumage. When in nuptial plumage the crown is completely black.

Whiskered Tern
Chlidonias hybrida

This is one of several birds known as marsh terns, but it is the only one that breeds in Australia. Of course this alternative name refers to the birds' habit of frequenting swamps, lakes and shallow flooded areas both salt and brackish; so much so that it is infrequently seen on the coast. Unlike the Caspian Tern which typically dives for fish the Whiskered Tern predominantly feeds by snatching fish, frogs, insects and crustaceans from or near the surface and will only occasionally dive.

Brolga
Grus rubicundus

Included in the world's fourteen species of crane, tall long-legged stately birds, are some of the most endangered species of larger birds on earth. The Sandhill Crane of America and eastern Siberia and the Manchurian Crane of Japan are examples that have come close to extinction in recent times. The Brolga, or Australian Crane (below), is also found in New Guinea, and was once recorded as a single vagrant bird to New Zealand. It comes as a shock to learn as recently as 1966 that another species of crane, the Sarus, *Grus antigone*, also occurs not uncommonly in tropical Australia. This bird is distinguished from the Brolga by its more extensive bare scarlet skin about the head, throat and upper neck.

The Brolga is far more numerous in the north of its range and is in fact uncommon and local elsewhere. It is a bird of shallow swamplands, flooded plains and grasslands and other open areas where it probes into mud with its dagger-like bill for sedge tubers, and also eats insects such as grasshoppers. Brolgas may be seen in very large flocks, particularly when the dry season reduces wetlands and birds must congregate on limited shallow water. Brolgas are well known for performing group dances during which birds leap about with extended wings whilst throwing the head back or bowing it downward, kicking the long legs out and calling. This is a ritualized courtship display but may also be seen performed outside the breeding season.

Pied Goose
Anseranus semipalmata

The black and white Pied or Magpie Goose (below), which also occurs in New Guinea, is to ornithologists the most remarkable waterfowl in Australia and has been given the distinction of its own subfamily. Its feet are only partly webbed and this is clearly an adaptation to the bird's way of life, as it commonly perches in trees and often walks considerable distances. This bird is also noteworthy for a conspicuous bulbous knob on its crown, which is usually larger in males. Another most odd anatomical development is found in adult males, which have a greatly lengthened windpipe extending in loops down the breast between the skin and breast muscles; so that it can be felt by touching the skin lightly. This remarkable development enables the birds to produce a very loud high pitched honking.

Masked Plover
Vanellus miles

The Masked Plover (opposite), is a familiar bird to all that live within its range. It is known to some by the appropriate name of Alarmbird, applied for its habit of leaping into flight and giving its sharp penetrating alarm call when it is approached too closely. It is a bird often to be seen in the suburban setting, on larger lawns, football pitches, golf courses and such situations as well as on swamplands. Pairs of birds are most aggressive when nesting, and will fly about calling and diving at people approaching the nest. Another name given to this bird is Spurwinged Plover, which refers to the frequently conspicuous spur on the leading edge and bend of the wing, which is used in display and fighting. At other times the spur is concealed by feathers.

White-headed Shelduck
Tadorna radjah

Also commonly known as the Radjah Shelduck or Burdekin Duck this lovely duck is very much a bird of the Australian tropics and is not very common anywhere readily accessible; as a result most people know it from captive birds in zoo collections. It frequents brackish waters and mud banks and estuaries of tropical rivers where it feeds upon worms, molluscs, insects and plant life. Freshwater lagoons and swamps are also frequented in the wet season and lagoons, swamps and lakes may be visited in the drier periods, but the vast majority of time is spent in brackish waters. These birds nest in large hollows in tree trunks or limbs near water and lay between six to twelve smooth cream coloured eggs onto the bare wood. Seen in this picture are nine young birds in the care of their parents.

Photo: T. & P. Gardner/A

Whistling Ducks

This photograph includes both the Diving Whistling and Plumed Whistling Ducks; the former are the darker breasted birds with black bills and crowns and the latter have a pale bill and crown, larger side plumes and chestnut sides to the breast with obvious black bars. Diving Whistling Ducks, *Dendrocygna arcuata*, are truly tropical in distribution whereas the Plumed Whistling Duck, *D. eytoni*, is rather more widespread (see maps above). Both are handsome long-legged and long-necked ducks which used to be referred to as tree-ducks because they perch. They do not perch as regularly as the name would imply, however, and so a name change was considered in the best interest of those dealing with the birds both nationally and internationally.

The Diving Whistling Duck feeds in deeper lagoon water by diving, the Plumed Whistling Duck does not dive but may dabble.

Green Pygmy Goose
Nettapus pulchellus

Another tropical species of waterfowl with a distribution similar to that of the Diving Whistling Duck. Green Pygmy Goose is a misnomer really for the bird is very much a duck and not a goose, but is doubtless so named for its stout goose-like beak used for grazing, as is the heavy bill of true geese. This beautiful duck is usually seen in pairs, or in small flocks. It frequents lakes, lagoons and other waters with good aquatic vegetation upon which it feeds both on the surface and by diving to submerged plants close to the surface. It nests both on the ground or in tree hollows beside water which the male will swim upon and defend whilst the female incubates the eight to twelve eggs.

oto: T. & P. Gardner/ANT

Black-fronted Dotterel
Charadrius melanops

This is undoubtedly one of the most familiar of birds to those bird-watchers frequenting wetland or river habitats with mud or gravel edges or banks. Striking plumage patterns, brilliant bill and bare eye ring skin, and a delightful habit of bobbing its head when standing alert, make it a particularly handsome little dotterel. In addition to occurring throughout most of Australia where suitable habitat exist, the bird has very recently established itself in New Zealand. It feeds upon small insects and aquatic animals.

49

Woodlands

oto: D. Hollands/ANT

51

Crested Hawk
Aviceda subcristata

This spectacular bird of prey (page 51) is of a predominantly tropical distribution in Australia, although it does extend down the east coast as far as the Sydney area. It also occurs in the Sunda Islands, Timor, the Moluccas and New Guinea to the Solomon Islands. This, the only crested Australian bird of prey, frequents woodlands, riverine forests, and rainforests. Despite its fierce appearance it feeds predominantly on insects in trees, but also takes amphibians, reptiles and small mammals.

Collared Sparrowhawk
Accipiter cirrhocephalus

Occurring throughout Australia, New Guinea and surrounding islands the Collared Sparrowhawk frequents a very wide range of habitats in addition to woodlands. Like its close but larger relatives, the goshawks, it is a superb and ferocious hunter of smaller birds sometimes taking birds larger than itself. Using vegetation as cover it flies at the prey with great speed and snatches it with the talon-tipped long yellow legs. This bird is seen alone or in pairs and can be found present in areas with the near identical, but larger, Australian Goshawk, *Accipiter fasciatus*.

Bar-shouldered Dove
Geopelia humeralis

Bar-shouldered doves prefer woodland with more shrub cover, and are thus more commonly found where woodland approaches other habitats such as pandanus swamp, melaleuca woodlands or mangroves; but they do occur in open woodland. In addition to the Australian tropics this bird is distributed throughout southern New Guinea and south-eastern Queensland and New South Wales. It is a bird that tends to associate with suitable habitats close to water. In the tropical part of its range it is a very common bird as its habitat has been relatively undisturbed by agriculture or industry, unlike in the south. This little pigeon is usually encountered in pairs or small parties but during the drier times of the year may form groups of more than a hundred. Food, consisting of seeds, is sought on the ground in open areas close to cover, to which the birds may flee.

Rainbow Lorikeet
Trichoglossus haematodus

This extremely colourful and noisy lorikeet is well known and much loved for its beauty throughout the eastern and south-eastern coastal region of Australia. In the northern region of the Kimberley and Arnhem Land it is replaced by the very similar, but little seen, Red-collared Lorikeet, *Trichoglossus rubritorquis*. These birds, being lorikeets, are unlike most parrots, which feed upon seeds, in that they feed predominantly upon flower nectar. As an adaptation for this diet they have a tongue that is 'brushed' at its tip to enable the bird to lap up nectar of flowers. Because the bill is not used for crushing seeds it is smaller and weaker than in other parrots. Birds do, however, eat some seeds as well as blossoms, fruits and insects. In addition to woodlands these birds frequent rainforests, scrublands, plantations, gardens and roadside trees.

Blue-winged Kookaburra
Dacelo leachii

Of all Australian birds Kookaburras require least introduction, being synonymous with the word Australia. These birds are of course giant kingfishers but are unlike the typical kingfishers in feeding habits as well as in appearance (see pages 28-29). Kookaburras feed upon a wide variety of prey including snakes, lizards, large insects, small mammals and the odd small bird. They also quickly adapt to living with man and the better known Laughing Kookaburra, *Dacelo gigas*, will feed upon garden scraps and become a problem at picnic areas where it will even pounce upon a piece of meat passing between plate and mouth. The Blue-winged Kookaburra can frequently be seen perched about the streets of tropical cities and towns, and within the range of the Laughing Kookaburra both species can be seen sitting on the same roadside wires. The Blue-winged is in fact the tropical species and is a more colourful bird, with extensive light blue areas on wing, rump and, in the male, blue tail. The tail of the female is red-brown with darker barring. Blue-winged Kookaburras do not have the amusing human-like laugh call of their close relative, but produce a more guttural raucous squawking and screeching. They occur in woodland, paperbark swamp and riverine vegetation.

Rainbow Bee-eater
Merops ornatus

Australia has only the single representative of the bee-eater family which world-wide consists of twenty-three colourful species. The Rainbow Bee-eater (opposite) is as lovely as most of the family members and also occurs in the Lesser Sunda Islands, New Guinea, the Bismarck Archipelago and the Solomon Islands. Unfortunately for the Tasmanians it does not occur on their island state, and is absent from the extreme southern parts of the continent. Many of the Australian birds, particularly in the south of their range, migrate to New Guinea for the winter whereas some northern birds are resident. In addition to woodlands, birds also frequent open country and may form huge night roosts in denser vegetation of heavy woodland, mangroves and rainforest. They nest by excavating a burrow into a bank or sandy soil and lay four to five eggs. The young are fed upon flying insects, the diet of adults.

Leaden Flycatcher
Myiagra rubecula

The photograph shows a male bird that has been collecting spiderwebs and other very fine material for the construction of a delicate small cupped nest which he assists the female in building. The nest is placed upon a horizontal limb and is stuck in place by the foundation of spiderwebs. The female differs from her mate in appearance quite markedly, being a dull lead-grey above, but browner on the back. Her throat is a pale orange-rufous becoming paler on the breast to meet the white underparts as in the male. These birds are very active as they seek their insect food in the foliage or fly into the air to snatch up a flying insect. Not confined to eucalypt woodland by any means this bird also occupies swamp woodlands, riverine forest and mangroves.

Northern Fantail
Rhipidura rufiventris

This fantail, confined to the northern tropics, is of course a very close relative of our very familiar Willie Wagtail, *Rhipidura leucophrys*, Grey Fantail, *R. fuliginosa*, and Rufous Fantail, *R. rufifrons*. It is in general appearance very similar to the Grey Fantail but it is larger, different about the head in pattern, and carries itself in a less typically fantail, more flycatcher-like, manner by perching more upright and fanning the tail less. The nest is typical of the fantails, being a delightful wine-glass shaped structure attached to a twig.

White-throated Honeyeater
Melithreptus albogularis

The White-throated is one of six very similar species of *Melithreptus* honeyeater but it is the one species whose distribution is predominantly tropical. This is a bird rarely photographed, as it feeds upon insects and flower nectar from the outer foliage of upper tree canopies. Its delicate cup-shaped nest is suspended from a fork of thin twigs above five metres high. It is usually encountered in pairs or small foraging parties, and in eastern Queensland it may be confused with the White-naped Honeyeater, *M. lunatus*, which, however, has an orange not pale blue patch of bare skin over the eye.

Yellow-breasted Sunbird
Nectarinia jugularis

This delightful bird is familiar to people living on the tropical east coast of Queensland, to which it is predominantly limited. It is the only Australian representative of the extremely colourful one hundred and eighteen species of sunbirds that occur from Africa through Asia to Australasia. Whilst the females, as can be seen in the photograph, are generally dressed in yellows and olives or browns the males are quite resplendent. The male Yellow-breasted is somewhat less gaudy than many other sunbirds, being like his mate but sporting a throat and breast of iridescent metallic blue-black. The tear-shaped suspended nest may often be found attached to a hanging piece of string or wire about the house or garden of a tropical town residence.

Gouldian Finch
Erythrura gouldiae

Few would argue with the suggestion that the Gouldian (opposite) is the loveliest of Australian, if not all, finches. Not only do birds appear with red faces as in the photograph, but other individuals have the face black and a few have a golden yellow face. This is a bird restricted to the northern tropics, but absent from the east coastal strip. During the wet season birds move to the southern part of their range, into drier woodland, and scrubland with grasses, but in the dry they frequent waterside vegetation and grassy areas in the north. This is but one of the eighteen grass finches native to Australia (see page 21).

Figbird
Sphecotheres viridis

The Figbird, which is also found in the eastern Lesser Sunda Islands, Timor and New Guinea, is a member of the oriole family but constitutes a bird so different from all other orioles that it is one of only three members of the family not in the genus *Oriolus* (see page 10). There are two forms of the figbird which were previously considered two distinct species, known as the Yellow and Southern Figbirds. The yellow form, as photographed, occurs in the north of the species' range and a green form is in the south. Both forms meet and intermingle to produce a mixed population about the Townsville area. As their name implies, these birds associate closely with figs as a food resource, but eat numerous other fruits and some insects. Outside the breeding season, when pairs raise two or three young, figbirds form flocks which may cover considerable distances and habitats in search of fruit.

Spangled Drongo
Dicrurus hottentottus

Drongo is a word widely used in Australia as slang for a fool or idiot, often by people who have never heard the word applied to the bird. Drongos in fact constitute a group of twenty very similar looking birds found from Africa through Asia to Australasia mostly within the tropics. Drongos feed upon flying insects which they search for by perching on an exposed branch and then chasing them skilfully in flight. The Spangled Drongo is usually seen as a lone bird or in pairs but occasional associations of more birds may be seen. Some proportion of this bird's Australian population migrates south for the winter, and others apparently migrate to and from New Guinea. This bird is sometimes known as fish-tail because of the peculiar shape of the tail. The bird seen here is sitting upon its nest.

Great Bowerbird
Chlamydera nuchalis

This bird is the largest of the eighteen bowerbirds, of which nine species are found in Australia (see page 23). It is a bird of the tropical eucalypt woodland, riverine vegetation and drier scrubs. As in the far better known Satin Bowerbird, *Ptilonorhynchus violaceus*, male Great Bowerbirds build 'avenue' bowers consisting of two parallel walls of sticks placed vertically into a mat or platform of sticks laid on the ground. This bower is constructed solely to impress potential mates, and to deter rival males who maintain bowers elsewhere for the same purpose. The males are promiscuous in their breeding and spend the breeding season calling and displaying at their bowers in an effort to mate with as many females as will accept them. The females will then nest build, incubate their one or two eggs, and raise their young entirely alone and unaided by the male. To enhance the attractiveness of his bower to the females the male decorates his bower area with bones, stones, fruits and man-made objects as can be seen in the photograph.

Fawn-breasted Bowerbird
Chlamydera cerviniventris

The Fawn-breasted Bowerbird is found only on the northern tip of the Cape York Peninsula in Australia, but also lives in some extensive coastal areas of New Guinea. It frequents eucalypt-melaleuca woodland, vine scrubs, riverine thickets, grasslands and mangrove fringes. Like the Great Bowerbird male Fawn-breasted Bowerbirds build 'avenue' bowers, but build their parallel vertical walls atop substantial raised platform-like piles of sticks (see photo). Unlike the Great Bowerbird which uses many stones and bones for decorations this bird uses predominantly green fruits.

Drylands

Emu
Dromaius novaehollandiae

The Emu is literally an Australian institution, appearing as it does on our national coat-of-arms and in being so very closely associated with the nation. It is another of the most primitive of bird groups, the ratites (see page 4). Emus are found over a great deal of Australia, but find the well vegetated areas of the east and south-eastern coasts unattractive, as they are very much birds of the open arid plains and scrubs, pastures and open woodlands. They are nomadic birds, walking over vast distances at times, in search of their omnivorous diet of grasses, leaves, flowers, fruits and insects.

When forced to do so Emus are capable of attaining speeds of about fifty kilometres an hour. Usually they would not require this ability but in their recent associations with man they have often been caused to try and escape death by the best means available to them in their flightless condition. Western cereal farmers see Emus as serious pests and will shoot them from vehicles. In 1932 the Australian army was dispatched with machine guns in an attempt to exterminate them in particular areas. Birds were herded by vehicles along fence lines and shot down as they ran parallel to the obstruction. Despite the ludicrous scale of this attempt it failed miserably, with only hundreds of birds being shot for the expenditure of many thousands of rounds of ammunition.

As in the Cassowary, it is the male Emu that incubates the eggs and cares for the young. Females lay five to twenty eggs, more usually about ten, in the nest scrapes of their mates and then leave the area. The male sits almost continuously for eight weeks until the chicks hatch; then cares for the young for as long as a year and a half until they are completely independent.

Wedge-tailed Eagle
Aquila audax

The Wedge-tailed Eagle is the largest bird of prey in Australia and, being of the genus *Aquila*, is a true Eagle as is the Golden Eagle of Eurasia and America. This is another bird to gain considerable advantage by white man's invasion of Australia in that it has provided water and carrion foods where much less or none at all were available. As is so often the case with large birds of prey, farmers convinced themselves without any real evidence that Wedge-tailed Eagles destroyed sheep and other valuable stock. Countless birds were shot or trapped and their corpses hung on fence lines in order to deter other birds, or impress passers-by. A long term scientific study proved, however, that not only do these magnificent birds only take sick or dying lambs and other useless stock, but that they kill numerous rabbits and thereby greatly assist the farmers.

Australian Bustard
Ardeotis australis

This heavy and stately bird was unfortunate enough to be both highly edible and easily shot when white man arrived and settled in Australia. Even today selfish people with no regard for our natural heritage shoot these birds which, save for exceptional circumstances, is completely unjustified and of course highly illegal. The other twenty-odd species of the bustard family, distributed throughout Africa, Eurasia and Indonesia have almost all suffered from human exploitation too. Indeed several are on the brink of extinction and a number are extinct over much of their previous range. Today the Australian bird is absent from much of what once was its natural distribution so that it is no longer to be found near heavily settled areas and few lightly settled ones. It inhabits grasslands and lightly timbered scrub and woodlands, where it feeds upon grasses, fruits and many large insects as well as small reptiles and mammals.

Fork-tailed Kite
Milvus migrans

The Fork-tailed, or Black, Kite (opposite) is a scavenger and a very well known one throughout its vast range of Europe, Asia, Africa, South East Asia and Indonesia to New Guinea and surrounding islands. It is a bird that has benefited much by human settlement, providing it with food and water in areas it would otherwise be unable to inhabit. Roads provide birds with an endless supply of carrion in the form of mammals, birds and insects hit by vehicles. In tropical Queensland the sugar cane fires, set each season to burn off unwanted dry foliage, provide convenient prey which can be looked for whilst soaring in the hot air thermals above the burning cane.

Australian Pratincole
Stiltia isabella

Of Australia's two species of pratincole, the Oriental is the truly tropical and more colourful representative, whilst the slightly drabber Australian Pratincole is distributed far more widely. The Oriental Pratincole is a migrant to Australia from its breeding ground in central and southern Asia and arrives here about October to December to remain until May. The Australian Pratincole is migratory within Australia with birds moving south-east to breed in spring and summer and returning northward for winter. It frequents open plains, claypans, floodplains and lagoon edges.

Bush Stone-curlew
Burhinus magnirostris

Most people in inland Australia are familiar with the haunting nocturnal wailing calls of this bird. It favours grassy areas with some woodland, with leaf litter and debris for cover. Nesting birds sit out the daylight hours by keeping perfectly still, crouching and relying upon cryptic plumage to conceal them. If approached closely they adopt a peculiar posture with head, neck, body and tail held flat against the ground to eliminate any profile or shadows. If approached closer a defence posture is performed (see photograph) which is followed by leaving the nest to challenge the intruder with wings outstretched in a defensive run. They feed upon various ground dwelling insects and other invertebrates.

Photo: R. & D. Keller/AN

Squatter Pigeon
Geophaps scripta

This sombrely coloured ground dwelling pigeon is predominantly confined to tropical Queensland where it frequents grassy plains, sparser woodlands and the modified country about homesteads and settlements. Indeed, this bird will quickly become very tame and confiding if regularly fed and not startled. Squatter Pigeons feed on the ground upon seeds and the odd insect.

Galah
Cacatua roseicapilla

This is another bird whose name is used to describe someone playing the fool or being stupid, and as a result Galah is literally an Australian household word. The bird is an extremely abundant and beautiful small species of cockatoo that is commonly kept as a pet. In captivity they will, if fed and treated properly, learn to speak and live for many years, sometimes longer than their owner. In the wild vast flocks may be seen on the ground feeding upon seeds, or in flight as a coloured cloud of grey and pink as seen here. This is a bird of open country with suitable nesting, feeding and perching trees.

Photo: T. & P. Gardner/ANT

Photo: R. & D. Keller/ANT

Photo: T. & P. Gardner/ANT

Grass Owl
Tyto longimembris

The lovely rare Grass Owl (opposite) is very similar to the very much more common and widespread Barn Owl, *Tyto alba*, with which it may be easily confused. Grass Owls are, however, rarely seen and have a much more restricted, and odd, distribution within Australia. Beyond our shores it occurs in India, South East Asia to New Guinea and Pacific Islands. Our birds dwell in grasslands or swampy areas, plains, heaths, sugar cane plantations and similar situations. The only other owls of predominantly tropical distribution are the Lesser Sooty Owl, *Tyto multipunctata*, of the Atherton Region rainforests and the huge Rufous Owl, *Ninox rufa*, of the northern and north-eastern tropical areas in closed forests.

Variegated Wren
Malurus lamberti

This variable and colourful wren, in which females are very much drabber, covers much of Australia; but is split into a number of forms or subspecies. The form present throughout most of Australia also inhabits the drier tropical zones in various habitats providing low undergrowth cover. A wren entirely confined to the tropics is the Lilac-crowned, *Malurus coronatus*, which is found only in the relatively inaccessible Kimberley and Gulf of Carpentaria areas. The Red-backed Wren, *M. melanocephalus*, is another tropical wren, which extends down the east coast into New South Wales.

Red-browed Pardalote
Pardalotus rubricatus

Pardalotes are five very attractive and colourful little birds confined to Australia; and at least one species is present somewhere throughout the country. The Red-browed is predominantly tropical, and is a bird of the drier inland woodlands and mulga. They are birds of the tree foliage, gleaning small insects from the eucalypt leaves. As in most pardalotes the nest is built within a chamber at the end of a tunnel excavated into a bank or earth cliff face.

Spotted Bowerbird
Chlamydera maculata

The Spotted Bowerbird is another of the 'avenue' bower building species of bowerbirds (see page 59) but is the member of the family that inhabits the drier and even very arid interior of Australia, including the dry tropics. Seen on page 68 is a male on his bower which is similar in form to that of the Great Bowerbird but is made from very much finer twigs, and grasses.

Further Reading

FORSHAW, J. M.
1981
Australian Parrots
Second Edition, Lansdowne, Melbourne

FRITH, C. & FRITH, D.
1992
Australia's Wet Tropics Rainforest Life
Frith & Frith Books, Malanda

FRITH, H. J.
1967
Waterfowl in Australia
Angus & Robertson, Sydney

FRITH, H. J.
1982
Pigeons and Doves of Australia
Rigby, Adelaide

HARRISON, C. J. O.
(Editor) 1978
Bird Families of the World
Elsevier – Phaidon, Oxford

HOLLANDS, D.
1984
Eagles, Hawkes and Falcons of Australia
Nelson, Melbourne

PIZZEY, G.
1980
A Field Guide to the Birds of Australia
Collins, Sydney

READERS DIGEST SERVICES
1976
Readers Digest Complete Book of Australian Birds
Readers Digest, Sydney

SERVENTY, V. N.
(Editor) 1982
The Wrens and Warblers of Australia
Angus & Robertson, Australia

SERVENTY, D. J., SERVENTY, V. N. & WARHAM, J.
1971
The Handbook of Australian Sea-Birds
Reed, Sydney

SIMPSON, K.
(Editor) 1984
The Birds of Australia
Lloyd O'Neil, Victoria

SLATER, P.
1970-1974
A Field Guide to Australian Birds, Non Passerines and Passerines
Two volumes. Rigby, Australia

Index to Birds